Francis Frith's
AROUND DERBY

◆

PHOTOGRAPHIC MEMORIES

Francis Frith's
AROUND DERBY

Clive Hardy

First published in the United Kingdom in 1999 by
Frith Book Company Ltd

Hardback Edition
ISBN 1-85937-046-2

Paperback Edition 2001
ISBN 1-85937-367-4

British Library Cataloguing in Publication Data

Francis Frith's Around Derby
Clive Hardy

Frith Book Company Ltd
Frith's Barn, Teffont,
Salisbury, Wiltshire SP3 5QP
Tel: +44 (0) 1722 716 376
Email: info@francisfrith.co.uk
www.francisfrith.co.uk

Printed and bound in Great Britain

As with any historical database the Frith archive is constantly being corrected and improved
and the publishers would welcome information on omissions or inaccuracies

CONTENTS

◆

FRANCIS FRITH: *Victorian Pioneer*

FRANCIS FRITH, Victorian founder of the world-famous photographic archive, was a complex and multitudinous man. A devout Quaker and a highly successful Victorian businessman, he was both philosophic by nature and pioneering in outlook.

By 1855 Francis Frith had already established a wholesale grocery business in Liverpool, and sold it for the astonishing sum of £200,000, which is the equivalent today of over £15,000,000. Now a multi-millionaire, he was able to indulge his passion for travel. As a child he had pored over travel books written by early explorers, and his fancy and imagination had been stirred by family holidays to the sublime mountain regions of Wales and Scotland. 'What a land of spirit-stirring and enriching scenes and places!' he had written. He was to return to these scenes of grandeur in later years to 'recapture the thousands of vivid and tender memories', but with a different purpose. Now in his thirties, and captivated by the new science of photography, Frith set out on a series of pioneering journeys to the Nile regions that occupied him from 1856 until 1860.

INTRIGUE AND ADVENTURE

He took with him on his travels a specially-designed wicker carriage that acted as both dark-room and sleeping chamber. These far-flung journeys were packed with intrigue and adventure. In his life story, written when he was sixty-three, Frith tells of being held captive by bandits, and of fighting 'an awful midnight battle to the very point of surrender with a deadly pack of hungry, wild dogs'. Sporting flowing Arab costume, Frith arrived at Akaba by camel seventy years before Lawrence, where he encountered 'desert princes and rival sheikhs, blazing with jewel-hilted swords'.

During these extraordinary adventures he was assiduously exploring the desert regions bordering the Nile and patiently recording the antiquities and peoples with his camera. He was the first photographer to venture beyond the sixth cataract. Africa was still the mysterious 'Dark Continent', and Stanley and Livingstone's historic meeting was a decade into the future. The conditions for picture taking confound belief. He laboured for hours in his wicker dark-room in the sweltering heat of the desert, while the volatile chemicals fizzed dangerously in their trays. Often he was forced to work in remote tombs and caves where conditions were cooler. Back in London he exhibited his photographs and was 'rapturously cheered' by members of the Royal Society. His reputation as a photographer was made overnight. An eminent modern historian has likened their impact on the population of the time to that on our own generation of the first photographs taken on the surface of the moon.

VENTURE OF A LIFE-TIME

Characteristically, Frith quickly spotted the opportunity to create a new business as a specialist publisher of photographs. He lived in an era of immense and sometimes violent change. For the poor in the early part of Victoria's reign work was a drudge and the hours long, and people had precious little free time to enjoy themselves.

Most had no transport other than a cart or gig at their disposal, and had not travelled far beyond the boundaries of their own town or village. However, by the 1870s, the railways had threaded their way across the country, and Bank Holidays and half-day Saturdays had been made obligatory by Act of Parliament. All of a sudden the ordinary working man and his family were able to enjoy days out and see a little more of the world.

With characteristic business acumen, Francis Frith foresaw that these new tourists would enjoy having souvenirs to commemorate their days out. In 1860 he married Mary Ann Rosling and set out with the intention of photographing every city, town and village in Britain. For the next thirty years he travelled the country by train and by pony and trap, producing fine photographs of seaside resorts and beauty spots that were keenly bought by millions of Victorians. These prints were painstakingly pasted into family albums and pored over during the dark nights of winter, rekindling precious memories of summer excursions.

THE RISE OF FRITH & CO

Frith's studio was soon supplying retail shops all over the country. To meet the demand he gathered about him a small team of photographers, and published the work of independent artist-photographers of the calibre of Roger Fenton and Francis Bedford. In order to gain some understanding of the scale of Frith's business one only has to look at the catalogue issued by Frith & Co in 1886: it runs to some 670

pages, listing not only many thousands of views of the British Isles but also many photographs of most European countries, and China, Japan, the USA and Canada – note the sample page shown above from the hand-written *Frith & Co* ledgers detailing pictures taken. By 1890 Frith had created the greatest specialist photographic publishing company in the world, with over 2,000 outlets – more than the combined number that Boots and WH Smith have today! The picture on the right shows the *Frith & Co* display board at Ingleton in the Yorkshire Dales. Beautifully constructed with mahogany frame and gilt inserts, it could display up to a dozen local scenes.

POSTCARD BONANZA

◆◆

The ever-popular holiday postcard we know today took many years to develop. In 1870 the Post Office issued the first plain cards, with a pre-printed stamp on one face. In 1894 they allowed other publishers' cards to be sent through the mail with an attached adhesive halfpenny stamp. Demand grew rapidly, and in 1895 a new size of postcard was permitted called the court card, but there was little room for illustration. In 1899, a year after Frith's death, a new card measuring 5.5 x 3.5 inches became the standard format, but it was not until 1902 that the divided back came into being, with address and message on one face and a full-size illustration on the other. *Frith & Co* were in the vanguard of postcard development, and Frith's sons Eustace and Cyril continued their father's monumental task, expanding the number of views offered to the public and recording more and more places in Britain, as the coasts and countryside were opened up to mass travel.

Francis Frith died in 1898 at his villa in Cannes, his great project still growing. The archive he created continued in business for another seventy years. By 1970 it contained over a third of a million pictures of 7,000 cities, towns and villages. The massive photographic record Frith has left to us stands as a living monument to a special and very remarkable man.

Frith's Archive: *A Unique Legacy*

FRANCIS FRITH'S legacy to us today is of immense significance and value, for the magnificent archive of evocative photographs he created provides a unique record of change in 7,000 cities, towns and villages throughout Britain over a century and more. Frith and his fellow studio photographers revisited locations many times down the years to update their views, compiling for us an enthralling and colourful pageant of British life and character.

We tend to think of Frith's sepia views of Britain as nostalgic, for most of us use them to conjure up memories of places in our own lives with which we have family associations. It often makes us forget that to Francis Frith they were records of daily life as it was actually being lived in the cities, towns and villages of his day. The Victorian age was one of great and often bewildering change for ordinary people, and though the pictures evoke an impression of slower times, life was as busy and hectic as it is today.

We are fortunate that Frith was a photographer of the people, dedicated to recording the minutiae of everyday life. For it is this sheer wealth of visual data, the painstaking chronicle of changes in dress, transport, street layouts, buildings, housing, engineering and landscape that captivates us so much today. His remarkable images offer us a powerful link with the past and with the lives of our ancestors.

TODAY'S TECHNOLOGY

Computers have now made it possible for Frith's many thousands of images to be accessed almost instantly. In the Frith archive today, each photograph is carefully 'digitised' then stored on a CD Rom. Frith archivists can locate a single photograph amongst thousands within seconds. Views can be catalogued and sorted under a variety of categories of place and content to the immediate benefit of researchers. Inexpensive reference prints can be created for them at the touch of a mouse button, and a wide range of books and other printed materials assembled and published for a wider, more general readership - in the next twelve months over a hundred Frith local history titles will be published! The

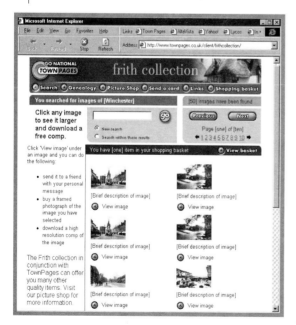

See Frith at www. francisfrith.co.uk

day-to-day workings of the archive are very different from how they were in Francis Frith's time: imagine the herculean task of sorting through eleven tons of glass negatives as Frith had to do to locate a particular sequence of pictures! Yet the archive still prides itself on maintaining the same high standards of excellence laid down by Francis Frith, including the painstaking cataloguing and indexing of every view.

It is curious to reflect on how the internet now allows researchers in America and elsewhere greater instant access to the archive than Frith himself ever enjoyed. Many thousands of individual views can be called up on screen within seconds on one of the Frith internet sites, enabling people living continents away to revisit the streets of their ancestral home town, or view places in Britain where they have enjoyed holidays. Many overseas researchers welcome the chance to view special theme selections, such as transport, sports, costume and ancient monuments.

We are certain that Francis Frith would have heartily approved of these modern developments, for he himself was always working at the very limits of Victorian photographic technology.

The Value of the Archive Today

Because of the benefits brought by the computer, Frith's images are increasingly studied by social historians, by researchers into genealogy and ancestory, by architects, town planners, and by teachers and schoolchildren involved in local history projects. In addition, the archive offers every one of us a unique opportunity to examine the places where we and our families have lived and worked down the years. Immensely successful in Frith's own era, the archive is now, a century and more on, entering a new phase of popularity.

The Past in Tune with the Future

Historians consider the Francis Frith Collection to be of prime national importance. It is the only archive of its kind remaining in private ownership and has been valued at a million pounds. However, this figure is now rapidly increasing as digital technology enables more and more people around the world to enjoy its benefits.

Francis Frith's archive is now housed in an historic timber barn in the beautiful village of Teffont in Wiltshire. Its founder would not recognize the archive office as it is today. In place of the many thousands of dusty boxes containing glass plate negatives and an all-pervading odour of photographic chemicals, there are now ranks of computer screens. He would be amazed to watch his images travelling round the world at unimaginable speeds through network and internet lines.

The archive's future is both bright and exciting. Francis Frith, with his unshakeable belief in making photographs available to the greatest number of people, would undoubtedly approve of what is being done today with his lifetime's work. His photographs, depicting our shared past, are now bringing pleasure and enlightenment to millions around the world a century and more after his death.

DERBY – *An Introduction*

THOUGH ONCE a major railway town, Derby was not created by the railways like Crewe and Swindon; it is a much older town, with a history going back to the Romans. The Roman station of Derventio guarded both a bridge over the Derwent and an important road junction, for it was here that the roads to Chester, Wall, Cirencester, Chesterfield, Buxton and York met. There were a number of small forts strung out along the roads of Cheshire and Derbyshire. These were used to secure lines of communication for the legionary bases at Chester and York, to police the local natives and to regulate the movement of salt and copper ore traffic from Cheshire and lead from the mines of Derbyshire. It might even be possible that Derventio had a mansio, a relay station for the imperial postal service, where messengers could either get accommodation or a change of horse. Nearby was a tribal village of the Coritani, and as far as we know local Britons and Roman auxiliaries appear to have co-existed reasonably well.

How long the fort remained in commission is unknown; it was still garrisoned in the mid-4th century. By then the Western Empire was in decline, torn apart from within by senseless civil wars as one general after another attempted to gain the purple, and threatened from without by barbarian incursions. There were a number of major troop withdrawals from Britain - by the usurper Magnus Maximus in AD383, by Stilicho in the AD390s and by Constantine III in AD407-11. Around AD395 a restructuring of the army took place, allowing the creation of a highly mobile field army of nine regiments, at least six of which were cavalry. As far as is known, the field army remained in Britain until the end.

At the beginning of the 5th century, Britain itself came under threat from Anglo-Saxon and Pictish raiders. A large part of the Roman garrison was away in Gaul fighting for Constantine III, emperor of Britain, against forces loyal to the imperial government and against barbarian invaders. The break with Rome finally came in AD410, the year the city of Rome itself fell to the Visigoths. The central Roman government would no longer take responsibility for Britain's defence or for its civil service. In response to an appeal from Britain for military assistance, the Emperor Honorious could only advise the province to look to its own defence; 350 years of direct imperial rule were at an end.

It is uncertain if any Roman troops left in Britain were withdrawn; we now know that many units, including those left on Hadrian's Wall, stayed behind. The Roman Army in Britain during the late-Roman period had little in common with that of the Claudian invasion; tactics, uniforms, equipment and recruitment had all changed. Many of the regiments had become 100 per cent British, as son followed father into the ranks to protect the land they and their relatives farmed, but they were still soldiers first. If orders were issued for a withdrawal, loyalty to the land

Mercians were centred on Tamworth, the North Mercians on Northworthy, the Anglo-Saxon name for Derby, or possibly an area that embraced Derby; but when the Mercian kingdoms united, Repton was chosen as their capital. We are still unsure where Northworthy was located in relation to the modern city, and several possible sites have been put forward.

For around three centuries the Anglo-Saxons were relatively free from outside interference, even if the various kingdoms seemed always to be at war with one another. Then in AD793 Danish raiders attacked the Northumbrian monastery on Lindisfarne

outweighed that to a crumbling empire either unwilling or unable to send troops their pay and provisions. Perhaps the troops at Derventio stayed behind, either to be destroyed by invading Angles or simply fading away into the local population to which they were almost certainly related.

By AD550 the Angles had established settlements at Chaddesden, Mackworth, and Alvaston, and by the 7th century the kingdoms of Mercia were established. The South

(Holy Island), ransacking the church for gold, killing monks, and enslaving anyone taken alive. It was the start of a hundred years of sporadic attacks. In AD867 the tactics changed. Instead of raiding and then leaving with their spoils, the Northmen wintered in England. From the AD870s the Danes, led by the likes of Guthrum and Halfdane, were no longer mounting raids, but were embarking on a campaign of conquest, taking the whole of East Anglia and a sizeable chunk of Mercia.

Under the terms of a treaty concluded between Guthrum and Alfred the Great, the conquered land became the Danelaw. Here the Danes were allowed to settle and Danish laws, not Anglo-Saxon, were followed. Northworthy, or Derby as we should now call it, became one of the Five Boroughs of the Danelaw; the others were Nottingham, Leicester, Lincoln and Stamford. Each of the Boroughs had its own 'army' council at which all freeholding landowners had a right to be heard.

Voting was done by a show of weapons, hence the old term wapentake for an administrative area. Each of the Five Boroughs could be expected to field several hundred troops, perhaps more. The townships themselves would have been built in the classic Danish style, narrow timber-framed houses and workshops with thatched roofs and wattle-and-daub walls. Again, we are not sure where the Viking settlement was situated.

The peace was always uneasy. In AD910 the Danes struck south in an all out attack to finish off the English kingdoms, but were stopped at Tettenhall by Edward the Elder of Wessex. Edward then went over to the offensive, his aim being the complete reconquest of the Danelaw. Edward's sister Aethelflaed, the widow of a Mercian earldorman, joined in the attack, her forces capturing Tamworth in AD913, which along with Stafford was then heavily fortified. Derby, as one of the principal burghs of the Danelaw, finally fell to Aethelflaed in AD918. The fighting at Derby was heavy. The Anglo-Saxon Chronicle tells us that Aethelfaed lost four of her thegns, all killed within the gates of Derby. This has led some people to believe that this means that the Danes used the old Roman fort. There are

precedents for the use of Roman fortifications: in tenth century York, for instance, the whole of the former legionary fortress was in use. But what we have to remember is that the old Danish word for street was gata, so the battle could have taken place somewhere else in the locality. Then again, the Danish settlement might well have comprised the old Roman fort and an additional ribbon development of wooden housing, workshops and warehouses stretching down to the banks of the Derwent, protected by ditch defences and palisades.

The war would continue for many years to come, but Derby was back in English hands for the time being. It was under Edward's successor Athelstan that for the first time there was a single country that could be identified as England, but it had had to be won by the sword and not by treaties. However, following Athelstan's death in AD939, the old animosities reappeared. Northumbria broke away, and there was open rebellion in what had been the Danelaw. In AD940 the Five Boroughs were in Viking hands, and the Northumbrian moneyer Rathulf was brought to Derby to strike coins with dies captured in the town.

In 1066 the town's population was somewhere around 1200, but by the time of the Domesday survey it had fallen to less than 700. There was probably more than one reason for this. Had Derby, like Cambridge, lost a large number of men at the Battle of Stamford Bridge, and possibly a few more at Hastings? Was the drop in population a direct result of William the Conqueror laying waste to the north? In any case, the town slowly recovered; by the end of the 14th century the population was around 3000.

In the 13th century one of the greatest fortresses in England was situated just a few miles to the north of Derby at Duffield. It belonged to Robert de Ferrers, Earl of Derby. In 1263 the earl rebelled against the king's authority and was defeated by Henry III. Though his possessions were ordered forfeit to the Crown, the earl was pardoned on condition that if he rebelled again he would be disinherited. In 1266, following the defeat of the barons at Evesham, Robert took to the field again, assembling a force at Duffield where he was joined by Baldwin de Wake, Lord of Chesterfield. On their way north to meet up with reinforcements from Yorkshire, the rebels were attacked by royal troops and forced to shelter behind the defences at Chesterfield. Prince Henry threatened to utterly destroy the town if Ferrers refused to surrender. The earl, who was suffering with gout, had hidden in the parish church behind some sacks of wool left by traders at the Whitsuntide fair: apparently at this time it was quite normal for churches to double up as warehouses. Ferrers was betrayed, captured and taken to Windsor in irons. The Ferrers estates were confiscated and Duffield Castle demolished.

Around 1278, Chesterfield merchants were able to grab a larger share of the lucrative market in lead at Derby's expense, thanks to the monks of Dale Abbey who obstructed the navigable Derwent with weirs at Borrowash. Chesterfield was able to offer an alternative route to London and the Continent via the port of Bawtry on the River Idle. It is possible that the Derbyshire lead mining industry of the late middle ages was operated on some sort of cartel basis. Many smelters and investors in mines were also merchants; in the 14th century the smelter Thurstan de Boure of Tideswell amassed a fortune operating bole hills and trading in lead at Chesterfield and Derby.

A bole hill was in effect a wind-assisted smelter. It was a walled enclosure a few feet in diameter with an opening facing the prevailing wind. It was filled with layers of timber or peat first, then lead ore. This was covered with more timber and then another layer of ore and so on until it was full, then it was topped off with turf. A channel ran from inside the bole to a gathering pool into which the molten lead would trickle. When the wind was in the right direction the bole was fired, and the smelted ore which collected in the gathering pool formed a pig of lead.

Breaking out in June 1348 and lasting until 1351, the Black Death swept through England and Scotland, leaving in its wake a decimated population. Recovery was hampered by further outbreaks in 1361-62, 1369 and 1375; these pushed the total fatalities to between

tres and their involvement in lead mining probably attracted an influx of survivors from decimated villages. Surviving documents show that throughout the country the period c1350 to 1450 was one of resettlement on an unprecedented scale, with people moving from one village to another and from village to town. Even so, the output of lead for the county as a whole fell to about half of what it had been in the 13th century, and in places like Ashford production ceased altogether.

DERBY AND THE '45

Derby's place in the political history of England was assured by the events of 1745-46. On 17th August 1745, Prince Charles Edward Stuart landed with a few loyal retainers on the shores of Glenfinnan at the head of Loch

one half and two-thirds of the entire population, and the effects would be felt for at least two centuries. Throughout the East Midlands, over four hundred villages were abandoned as a result of the Black Death and changes of settlement. Even so, the populations of Chesterfield and Derby may have held up reasonably well; their importance as textile cen-

Shiel. He had come to Scotland to raise the clans for an attempt to retake the throne for the House of Stuart. After three hours, only 150 men of Clan Ranald had joined him. Then Cameron of Lochiel turned up with 700 clansmen, followed by the MacDonalds of Keppoch. The Royal Standard was raised and the fight was on.

On 29th November, Prince Charles Edward and his followers entered Manchester. The town was considered important, so the Prince rode into town wearing his light tartan plaid, blue sash and blue bonnet. Once he had entered Lancashire, Charles had hoped for some tangible signs that the English Jacobites would rise. A few recruits had come in at Preston, but it was only at Manchester that they joined in any number, and even then it was only two hundred or so. Together with the recruits from Preston, these men were formed into the Manchester Regiment under the command of Francis Townley of Townley Hall. The Manchester Regiment were little better than a rabble and of little fighting value, but it was a start and others might yet join.

Charles was determined to carry on towards London. His experienced field commanders believed that Charles should quit while he was ahead and return to Scotland, but they agreed to continue as far as Derby, which like Lancashire was supposed to be a hotbed of support for the Stuart cause. On 3rd December the Jacobites reached Ashbourne, where the Prince stayed overnight at the home of the Cockayne family; on the following day he was entertained to lunch at Radbourne Hall. Meanwhile, it is possible that panic was beginning to grip the gentry of Derby. The town had raised a volunteer force, which together with a company raised by the Duke of Devonshire added up to about 880 men. They were drawn up in the Market Place and reviewed by the Duke of Devonshire, and were simultaneously plied with strong drink courtesy of the mayor and a number of other gentleman. On hearing that the rebel army was approaching, our gallant

lads decided that withdrawal was the better part of valour and headed off in the general direction of Nottingham, along with the local gentry and their families.

The advance party of the Jacobite army reached Derby at about eleven in the morning; the Prince himself arrived at dusk and took up residence at Exeter House. Any hopes of the English Jacobites joining the cause were soon dashed; though it used to be thought that only three Derby men enlisted, recent research has turned up a fourth name.

With two Hanoverian armies approaching, a Council of War was held. The Prince's field commanders were deeply concerned at both the lack of support from English Jacobites, and the doubt that a French invasion planned to support the venture would take place. At a second Council of War Charles agreed to abide by a majority decision on what to do next. The decision was taken to turn back, though an advance force had secured Swarkestone Bridge and the causeway over the Trent. In 1745, crossing the Trent was a potential tactical nightmare for any army, for there were few bridged crossing points. In securing Swarkestone, the Prince's army had gained an advantage but were unable to exploit it. Morale amid the ordinary clansmen was high. They had not yet been defeated in battle, so when the army left Derby on Friday 6th December, the Highlanders were told that they were heading south when in fact they were heading back north.

The southward advance had been met with the ringing of bells, bonfires, grand balls and proclamations. Returning north was something else. On entering Manchester they were booed and jeered at, and some citizens even thought about 'having a go' at the

Highlanders; not a wise move, considering the clansmen's formidable reputation at close-quarter fighting.

The fate of the Manchester Regiment was also sealed. Left to garrison Carlisle, the regiment was eventually forced to surrender without terms. For its survivors, retribution was indeed swift and in some cases positively barbaric. Many of the men were transported to

gramme. John had recently returned from Italy, where he had worked long enough to be able to steal the designs for their silk-throwing machinery. By 1732 the Derby Silk Mill was employing three hundred workers; the first factory in England. As for John, it is said that he was the victim of a contract killing, courtesy of his former Italian employers.

Another early factory in the town opened

the West Indies, the officers were executed as traitors; the heads of Thomas Deacon, Thomas Syddall and Lieutenant Chadwick were sent to Manchester to be exhibited on the Old Exchange. Thomas Townley's head was eventually returned to his family and placed in a specially prepared niche in the wall of their chapel at Townley Hall, where his widow could gaze upon it in private.

THE AGE OF INDUSTRY

By the middle of the 18th century framework knitting around Derby was specialising in silk hose, and by 1717 a mill established by Thomas Cotchett had been taken over by one of his former apprentices, John Lombe, and was undergoing a rapid expansion pro-

in 1756 for the manufacture of porcelain. Thanks to Royal patronage, it became known by the title of Crown Derby in 1773. The works closed in 1848, but in 1849 William Locke opened a new porcelain factory in King Street. In 1876 the Derby Crown Porcelain Co was floated, eventually opening up in what had been the local workhouse and known to the natives as the Bastille. In 1891 the company changed its name to the Royal Crown Derby Porcelain Co.

It was the coming of the railways in general and the selection of Derby by the Midland Railway for its headquarters in particular that transformed an obscure and insignificant county town into a major industrial centre. The Midland came into being in May 1844, an amalgamation of three railway companies operating in and out of the town. Amalgamation had been the sensible way out of a damaging price-cutting war that was being waged by the companies; a war none was likely to win. Derby was the natural choice for the headquarters and main workshops of the new company, and under Matthew Kirtley the works were transformed. As well as continuing with repairs and maintenance, Kirtley oversaw an expansion programme that gave Derby the capacity to construct locomotives. In 1851, goods engine No 147 was rolled out of the erecting shop, the first of over 2,900 new steam locomotives that would be built there. By 1862 the workshops were employing over 2,000 people, and as early as 1880 the Midland Railway had a telephone link with London.

Derby was growing fast. The last Derby-to-Manchester mail coach had run on 3 November 1855, with the driver William Burditt arriving at The Bell in Sadlergate at 4.00pm. The town was now a major railway centre, and this in turn had encouraged other businessmen to open factories, including Qualcast in 1849, Fletchers in 1860, and Leys Castings in 1870. In 1881 the dry-air refrigeration system developed in Derby by Alfred Haslam enabled cargoes of fresh beef and mutton to be brought from Australia, and in 1906 Rolls-Royce opened their factory at Osmaston Road. However, the town was rather late in getting its streets lit by arc lamps. That did not happen until 1893, some twelve years later than Chesterfield. However, the corporation power station was one of the first in the country to use steam turbines.

It is often forgotten that Derby was an early player in the tourist industry, thanks to Thomas Cook of Melbourne. The business

started out of Cook's work for the temperance movement; his first excursion took the friends of temperance from Leicester to Loughborough and back. Derby was used as the meeting-point for tourists from the south, south-west, south-east, East Anglia and Lincolnshire booked on his Scottish tours. Those needing overnight accommodation were housed at Smithard's Temperance Hotel in the Corn Market or by Cook himself at Leicester.

Simeon Smithard was Cook's half-brother and a reformed drunkard, who was later appointed agent for the South Midland Temperance Association. The following morning the train would depart from Derby, picking up at Chesterfield, Sheffield, Normanton, York (where a stop was made for a meal), Newcastle and Berwick.

Travelling on one of Cook's tours could be interesting, to say the least. On one trip, two coaches were derailed after the train collided with a horse on the line. The passengers attended to the injured guard, manhandled the carriages back onto the track, and off they went; no Railtrack investigation necessary. On one return trip, the passengers got the chance to have a quick look round Berwick while railway staff attempted to put out one of the carriages that had caught fire. Later that same morning, the engine driver just managed to stop the train from colliding with a coal train at Newcastle.

Of the 6,009,048 people who visited the Great Exhibition of 1851, 165,000 of them got there and back thanks to Thomas Cook. Despite initial reservations from the establishment, the Exhibition proved a hit with the workers. In the three months prior to its opening, Cook toured major industrial towns encouraging the forming of Exhibition Clubs so that members could save for their trip by making weekly contributions. Once the Exhibition was on, Thomas would send his son John from Derby to somewhere like Leeds or Bradford on a Friday with several trains of empty carriages. John then toured the streets in a van accompanied by a band, and persuaded the workers to part with five shillings each for their train fares. It is said that the local pawnshops were full of watches, the property of workers raising a little extra cash for spending money. John was later responsible for organising the first excursion to Alton Towers. The Earl of Shrewsbury was expecting a few hundred visitors: John turned up with 10,000.

No Ref, No Linesmen, No Offside Trap

Derby was also one of those places where Shrovetide football was played through the streets. Rules were few and far between, and it was parish against parish. On Shrove Tuesday the pancake bell was rung at mid-day; the players, probably numbering several hundred, descended upon the Market Place, where the ball was thrown up. Mayhem then ensued. It was not unusual for players to finish up with broken arms or legs, and if the ball went into the river or one of the brooks that flowed through the town, the players simply followed.

On Ash Wednesday the game was repeated, but this time restricted to those considered too young to play on Shrove Tuesday. A French prisoner of war, who happened to be in Derby during one of these games, wrote 'If the English call this playing, it would be impossible to say what they call fighting'. Still, there were plenty of self-important people around who wanted the game banned altogether, none more so than killjoy mayor William Mousley. Using heavy-handed powers, Mousley declared that it was forbidden to bring the ball into the Market Place; he even called in the cavalry to assist. Unfortunately, he had not reckoned with the natives. Little old Mother Hope hobbled into the Market Place, whipped the ball from under her skirts, and threw it up. In 1845 the corporation introduced two days of sports in its attempts to suppress the game, but allowed a modified game of football to take place on the understanding that it was not to be played in the streets. Alas, the game was finally banned in 1860, though on 1 March 1870 a football was thrown up in the traditional manner in Agard Street; following ancient custom, it was soon in the brook.

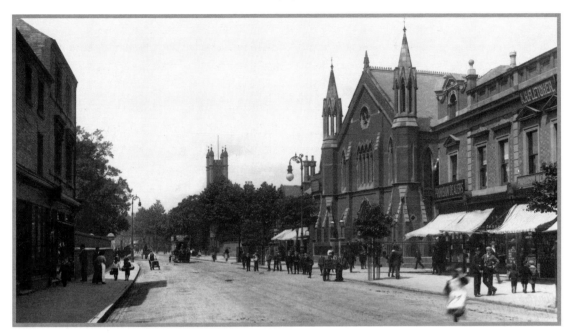

LONDON ROAD 1896 37781
The tower of Holy Trinity Church peers above a tree-lined and relatively traffic-free London Road. This particular church was built as a private development in 1836 under the name of St George's; the interior was painted red, white and blue. The builder went bankrupt and the church was eventually sold and renamed.

THE ROYAL INFIRMARY 1896 37787
The original Royal Infirmary was founded in 1806, and was designed by William Strutt to incorporate his patent air-duct central heating system. In 1891 work began on a much larger hospital complex; the town's population was continuing to grow rapidly and new medical facilities were desperately needed. The new infirmary buildings were officially opened by Edward VII in 1906.

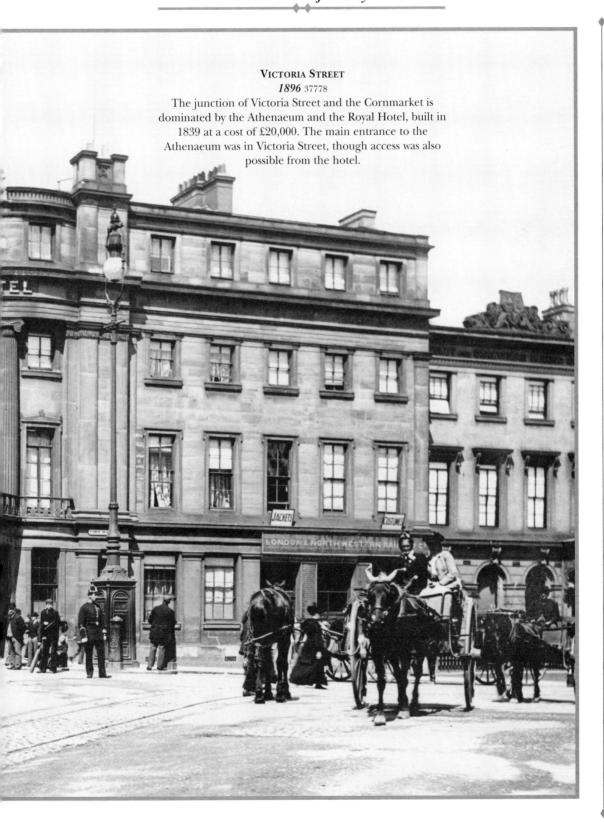

VICTORIA STREET
1896 37778
The junction of Victoria Street and the Cornmarket is
dominated by the Athenaeum and the Royal Hotel, built in
1839 at a cost of £20,000. The main entrance to the
Athenaeum was in Victoria Street, though access was also
possible from the hotel.

ST PETER'S CHURCH C1960 D24062
St Peter's Church on the junction of East Street, St Peter's Street and St Peter's Churchyard. On the left is the rather splendid local branch of Boots the Chemists, designed in the half-timbered style. Also along East Street was the Midland Drapery, founded by Edwin Ann in 1882 and which grew to become one of the town's principal stores.

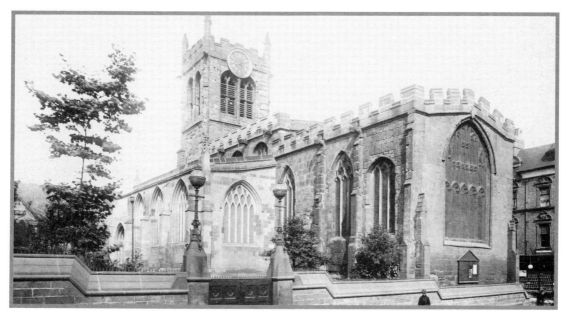

ST PETER'S CHURCH 1896 37786
The inhabitants of St Peter's parish used to take part in the local Shrovetide football matches against All Saints'. There were hundreds of players on each side, rules were few and far between and the playing area was the streets of the town. All Saints' goal was a waterwheel at Nuns Mill which had to be knocked three times for a goal to count. St Peter's goal was a nursery gate about a mile out of town.

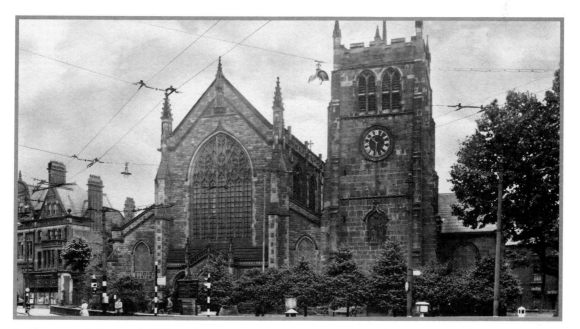

ST WERBURGH'S CHURCH C1955 D24025
In November 1322 there was something of a crisis for parishioners at St Werburgh's. Hugh Meynell of Langley was adjudged by the Bishop of Lichfield to have shed blood in the church. In those superstitious days, divine services would have had to be suspended until an inquisition had been held to prove whether or not blood had been spilt by violent means. Repentance would be necessary, usually the payment of a fine.

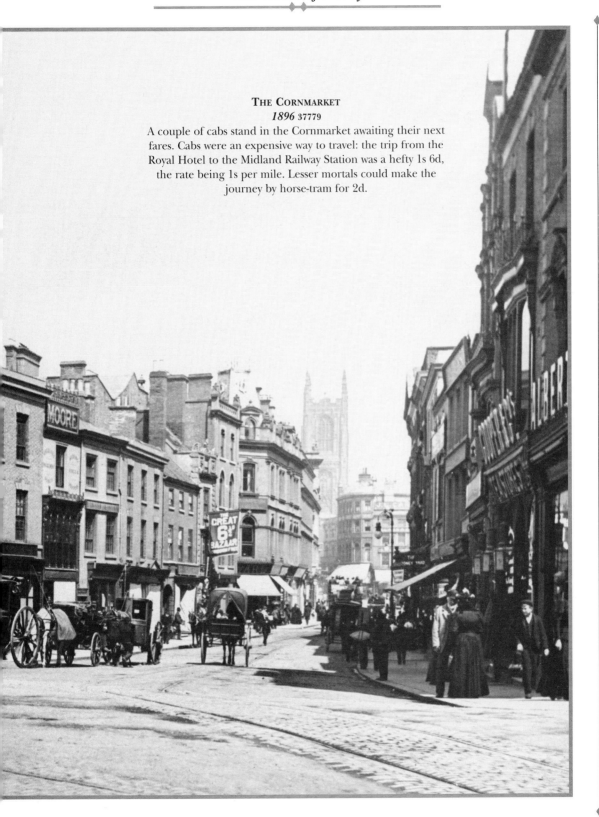

THE CORNMARKET
1896 37779
A couple of cabs stand in the Cornmarket awaiting their next
fares. Cabs were an expensive way to travel: the trip from the
Royal Hotel to the Midland Railway Station was a hefty 1s 6d,
the rate being 1s per mile. Lesser mortals could make the
journey by horse-tram for 2d.

THE TOWN HALL 1896 37776A
Electric street lighting came to Derby in 1891; the Market Place and Cornmarket were the first areas to be converted from gas lamps. The horse-trams started running in the 1880s, providing a link between the Midland and Great Northern railway stations; they survived until 1904, when they were replaced by electric trams.

THE TOWN HALL 1896 37776
In 1828 Derby's third Town Hall was officially opened. It was an elegant building complete with a grand porticoed entrance off the Market Place, but it only survived for twelve years before being destroyed by fire. The Guildhall was built in its place, opening in 1842.

THE CENOTAPH C1955 D24012
The Cenotaph is seen here through the entrance archway of the Guildhall and Market Hall. In those days the Market Place was the main terminus for the majority of bus routes operated by the council; the bus station was reserved for Trent, Bartons, Felix and Blue Bus services, as well as through coaches and tour buses.

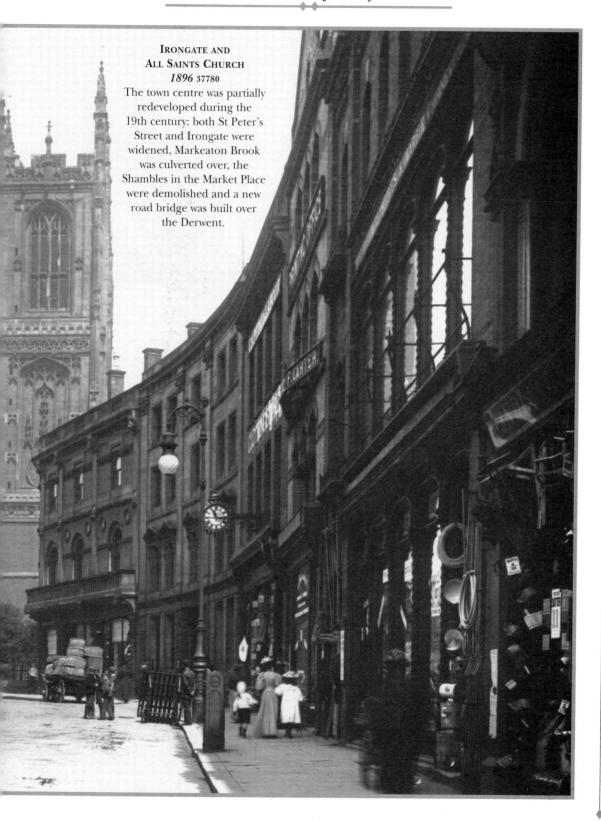

**IRONGATE AND
ALL SAINTS CHURCH
1896 37780**
The town centre was partially
redeveloped during the
19th century: both St Peter's
Street and Irongate were
widened, Markeaton Brook
was culverted over, the
Shambles in the Market Place
were demolished and a new
road bridge was built over
the Derwent.

IRONGATE AND THE CATHEDRAL c1955 D24011

On the 8th and 9th October 1831 the citizens of Derby rioted, angry at the failure of the Reform Bill on its final vote. Damage was done to houses and business premises of known anti-reformers; the door of the borough gaol was battered in and the prisoners released. In Irongate, Surgeon Henry Haden attempted to calm things down, but he was pushed to the ground; those going to his assistance found he was dead. The inquest returned a verdict of natural causes.

ST MARY'S BRIDGE c1960 D24055

Following a tip-off, a raid was mounted on Padley Hall in June 1588 and two Catholic priests, Robert Ludlam and Nicholas Garlick, were discovered in hiding. The unfortunate men were brought to Derby and hanged, drawn and quartered. Their dismembered bodies were displayed on poles on the approaches to St Mary's Bridge.

ALL SAINTS' CHURCH 1896 37783

In 1723 Dr Michael Hutchinson, the incumbent of All Saints', was having trouble with his parishioners. Hutchinson wanted to rebuild the church, which to be fair to him was in a bad state of repair, but the parishioners and the corporation objected. Not to be outdone, the resourceful Hutchinson acted independently: on the night of 18th February 1723 he had the roof ripped off and the interior demolished. There was little alternative but to rebuild, but Hutchinson had to raise the money himself through public subscription.

ST MARY'S CHURCH 1896 37793

St Mary's Roman Catholic Church was designed in the Victorian Gothic style by Augustus Pugin. Work began on the £7000 project in June 1838, and the dedication took place in October 1839. The town's Catholic community had been growing steadily since the Napoleonic Wars owing to large numbers of Irish immigrants attracted by the prospect of work in local mills.

St Alkmund's Church 1896 37785
Built in 1846 at a cost of £9,000 on the site of an earlier church, St Alkmund's is named after the son of the deposed Northumbrian king Alured. Alkmund was martyred in AD800 on the orders of King Eardulph and is said to have eventually been buried at Derby.

ST ALKMUND'S CHURCH 1896 37784
When St Alkmund's was demolished to make way for the inner ring road, archaeologists had an opportunity to excavate the site for the remains of the old Saxon church. Its foundations revealed a basic two-cell church of not later than the 9th century. St Alkmund's might well have been the church of Saxon Northworthy.

FROM THE DERWENT 1896 37789

In this photograph we see the tower of St Mary's and the spire of St Alkmund's. Partially hidden by the trees on the right is the chapel of St Mary's-on-the-Bridge. There was an earlier church dedicated to St Mary, given to Burton Abbey by William the Conqueror, but it does not appear to have survived for long.

MUNICIPAL BUILDINGS AND RIVERSIDE GARDENS c1955 D24017

Part way along the steps can be seen the culvert where Markeaton Brook surfaces to join the Derwent. At one time the brook was little better than an open sewer that meandered its way through town; a local name for it was Shitte Brook. The cells of the old town gaol were situated below the brook's flood level and some prisoners are known to have been drowned during flash floods. Others died of gaol fever.

THE ARBORETUM 1896 37792

THE ARBORETUM 1896

The Arboretum was given to Derby thanks to the generosity of Joseph Strutt, who donated the land and hired the top landscape designer of the day, John Loudon, to create a park planted with every tree and shrub capable of standing the climate. There were three days of celebrations to mark the opening; interest in the park was such that the Midland Railway Co ran excursion trains.

THE ARBORETUM 1896

The ornamental fountain and fishpond situated at the centre of the Arboretum. Loudon's design made use of irregular paths and undulating mounds to make the park appear much bigger than it actually was. Visitors to the Arboretum had to pay an entrance fee. However, in 1882 it was made free, though visitors were expected to wear their Sunday best.

THE ARBORETUM 1896 37790

MARKEATON PARK C1960 A200027

In 1895 the Mundy family donated land for this, the town's second park; Bass's Recreation Ground had opened in 1867, but it was not laid out as a park. Osmaston Park opened in 1922, followed by Darley Park in 1929 and Allestree Park in 1948.

MARKEATON PARK C1960 D24058

It took a serious flood in April 1842 to galvanise the corporation into action and order the culverting of Markeaton Brook. In May 1932 over £400,000 worth of damage was done in the town centre when a section of the culverting collapsed following heavy rain and the area flooded. A gas main in the Cornmarket was damaged by flood water and exploded, destroying the premises of H Samuels in the process.

MARKEATON HALL, THE LAKE C1960 D24057

Markeaton Hall, the seat of the Mundy family, was built in 1755. During the Reform Bill Riots which swept the town in 1831, the mob broke into the gaol in Friargate and released all the prisoners. Lady Mundy, fearing that Markeaton would be attacked, did not undress for four days and nights. Though the Hall has been demolished, its orangery and stables are still extant.

MICKLEOVER C1955 M220001

Thomas Cotchett was born at Mickleover before the Civil War; it was he who first brought silk-throwing machines to Derby when he imported some Dutch equipment. Cotchett employed George Sorocold to erect the machines in a mill situated on an island in the Derwent behind Full Street. One of the mill apprentices was John Lombe; Cotchett's mill later formed the basis for Lombe's Silk Mill.

MICKLEOVER, UTTOXETER ROAD c1955 M220050

MICKLEOVER
Uttoxeter Road c1955

The A516 Uttoxeter Road was notorious for slow moving traffic, and things only got better when a section of the A38 was made into a dual carriageway. This helped to speed things up for traffic either going to or coming from the Stoke and Burton directions.

◆

FINDERN
The Church c1965

Situated to the south-west of Derby, the village of Findern was once an outlier of Mickleover along with Littleover and Potlock. The lands were granted to Burton Abbey by William I, having been assessed by the Domesday commissioners as being worth £25 a year in taxes in 1066, but only £10 by 1085.

FINDERN, THE CHURCH c1965 F127002

REPTON, HIGH STREET
c1955 R298026
It is hard to imagine that Repton was once the capital of
Mercia, the burial place of kings and saints alike. During the
winter of AD874-75 a Viking army, perhaps 2500-3000 strong,
wintered at Repton instead of returning home. It was the
beginning of the end of Mercian control over the East
Midlands; the Danelaw would soon be a reality.

REPTON, THE SCHOOL c1955 R298001

A priory of the Black Canons was founded in Repton during the 12th century and survived until the Dissolution. Sir John Port incorporated some of the surviving buildings into Repton School, which he founded in 1556; this photograph shows the original arched gateway of the priory.

REPTON, ST WYSTAN'S CHURCH c1955 R298036

St Wystan's was built about AD975, and was extensively altered during the 13th to 15th centuries. Repton was the old capital of the Mercian kingdom, and a monastery was founded here in AD653 which was destroyed by the Danes during their conquest of the area some two hundred years later. The Anglo-Saxon crypt under St Wystan's dates back to the 7th century.

REPTON, FOREMARK HALL c1955 R298030

Foremark Hall is situated two miles east of Repton and five miles south of Derby. The Hall was built in the Palladian style by D Hiorns; the village church, dedicated to St Saviour, contains ironwork thought to be by Robert Bakewell.

CASTLE DONINGTON, BONDGATE c1955 C430012

Castle Donington is less than ten miles from the centre of Derby. The picture was taken when Trent Motor Traction still operated a parcels service, the country was hit with a series of newspaper and docks strikes and income tax was reduced by 6d in the pound.

CASTLE DONINGTON, MARKET STREET c1955 C430005
St Edward's church dates from the 13th and 14th centuries; there is a tombstone from about 1320 and brasses of Robert de Staunton and his wife. Staunton Harold itself passed into the hands of the Shirley family in 1423 on the marriage of Margaret de Staunton to Ralph Shirley.

CASTLE DONINGTON, BONDGATE C1955 C430004

The days of the Bondgate Cafe and Offilers' on draft at the Turk's Head are recalled here. Offilers' brewery was situated off Normanton Road, Derby, the company supplying a large number of pubs both in the town and surrounding areas. Alas its all gone, though the Nag's Head at Castle Donington can still offer the beer drinker such delights as Marston's and Banks's.

CASTLE DONINGTON, KINGS' MILL C1955 C430007

The Kings' Mill is a derelict 16th century paper mill on the Trent adjoining Donington Hall. It was to the Hall in 1919 that the German naval officers who had organised the scuttling of the High Seas Fleet in Scapa Flow were brought, interrogated and tortured.

ASHBOURNE
The Green Man 1886 18577

ASHBOURNE
Church Street c1955 A66020

The view down Church Street towards St Oswald's. On the left is the
famous Green Man & Black's Head, an old coaching inn
frequented by Dr Samuel Johnson (1709-84) and his drinking compan-
ion James Boswell (1740-95). Johnson usually stayed at the Mansion
House, owned by an old school friend of his, Dr Taylor. It was Taylor
who performed Johnson's burial service at Westminster Abbey.

ASHBOURNE, ST OSWALD'S CHURCH 1896 37875
St Oswald's was built in the decorated style, with high arcades, large windows and wide aisles. It was consecrated in 1241 and dedicated to Oswald, the second Northumbrian king to embrace Christianity, who was killed by Penda of Mercia in AD642. One of the church's famous monuments is the Carrara marble figure of five-year-old Penelope Boothby who died in 1791.

ASHBOURNE, THE MARKET PLACE 1957 A66018
In the 1990s the buildings remain very much the same, though some of the businesses are long gone. The porticoed Town Hall is in the middle of the block. Once a small market town, Ashbourne has become a fashionable place to live for those wishing to escape the urban sprawl of Derby.

ASHBOURNE, GENERAL VIEW c1955 A66045
Ashbourne is one of only two towns where the ancient game of Shrovetide football is still played; the other is Atherstone in Warwickshire. At Ashbourne it is played on both Shrove Tuesday and Ash Wednesday; these days the ball is thrown up from a special stand in Shaw Croft car park located behind the Green Man Inn.

DUFFIELD, THE RIVER AND THE CHURCH c1950 D159018

DUFFIELD, THE PARISH CHURCH c1965 D159007

DUFFIELD
The River and the Church c1950

On 6 August 1673 a levy was made on the townships of the parish to raise £83.10.5d 'for the repayre of the church of Duffield being much decayed by reason of a late flood'.

◆

DUFFIELD
The Parish Church c1965

The church is dedicated to St Alkmund. There was probably a wooden church on this site in Saxon times, as the Domesday Book mentions a priest at Duffield. Some traces of the Norman church remain, but the building appears to have been rebuilt during the 14th century. In 1847 it underwent an extensive rebuild when the north and south aisles were given high-pitched roofs.

DUFFIELD, THE BRIDGE OVER THE DERWENT c1950 D1593092

It was near here on 10th April 1673 that Robert Randall of Denbigh met with an unfortunate accident. Robert was staggering home after a day of boozing, brawling and betting at a cockfight in Duffield when he fell into the river and drowned.

DUFFIELD, TOWN STREET c1955 D159020

Robert de Ferrers, Fourth Earl of Derby, once held Duffield Castle, one of the greatest fortresses in 13th century England, as well as the castles at Tutbury and Oakham. It is said that in the days of William de Ferrers a Syrian variety of daffodil was introduced to Duffield, brought back from the Holy Land by a soldier.

DUFFIELD, TOWN STREET
c1955 D1593090

This view is still much the same today. By the side of Tamworth Street is an old stone bridge over the River Ecclesbourne which was made from stone salvaged from the castle ruins. All that remains of the fortress are the foundations of the keep.

DUFFIELD, GENERAL VIEW c1950 D159017

DUFFIELD, GENERAL VIEW c1950
This particular view was probably taken by Friths for their postcard range. Friths had been producing postcards since the 1880s, when postcards had to be placed inside an envelope for posting. In 1894 the Post Office agreed to allow them to be posted without an envelope at half the letter rate, but they could not carry any form of message; this rule remained in force until 1902.

◆

MILFORD, GENERAL VIEW c1955
Edward Smith of Milford was just six years old when he went to work for George Brettle's hosiery business in Belper. Eighty-six years later, Edward was still working at Brettle's, though the company felt that it was time he retired. Edward was offered a generous pension, but he immediately turned it down, threatening to leave and find another job.

MILFORD, GENERAL VIEW c1955 M354007

MILFORD, THE RIVER c1955 M354001

Jedediah Strutt's cotton mill at Milford was built in 1780 and was of an advanced design: it included a patent ducted-air central heating system invented by his son William. As there was no police force, Jedediah also raised the Milford Militia to protect his property from attack.

BELPER, HERBERT STRUTT SCHOOL c1955 B437037
Until Forster's Education Act which made education compulsory for all children between the ages of five and ten, things had been left in the hands of charities or the benevolence of wealthy patrons. Jedediah Strutt incorporated a schoolroom in the attic of the North Mill; his son Joseph was involved with the Lancastrian School for Boys which opened in Derby in 1812.

BELPER, BRIDGE STREET 1955 B437019
Belper was originally called Beaurepaire, after its pleasant location on the banks of the River Derwent. The earliest industry appears to have been nail making, the first recorded instance being in 1313, but this eventually died out during the 19th century.

BELPER, STRUTT'S MILLS C1955 B437006
Strutt's mills were built on both sides of the road to Ashbourne, and were linked by a bridge known as the gangway, which can be seen in the middle distance. To the left of the gangway were the West Mill (1795-96), the Reeling Mill (1808), and the Round Mill (1811). To the right was Strutt's first mill built in 1776, the North Mill (1786) and the East Mill (1912).

BELPER, EAST MILL C1955 B437015
The East Mill was the last addition to the complex. It was completed in 1912, by which time Belper's population was around 11,000, a far cry from Jedediah Strutt's day. Though Jedediah was a considerate employer who provided housing, a school and even a cottage hospital for his workers, he does not appear to have had any qualms about employing young children in his mills to clean the machinery.

BELPER, THE WEIR c1955 B437040
The original weir was constructed in 1775-76 to serve Strutt's first mill. In order to provide sufficient water for the ever growing complex, the Horseshoe Weir was built across the main channel of the Derwent in 1797.

BELPER, RIVERSIDE GARDENS c1955 B437002
The riverside gardens at Belper are well known to the locals but often missed by visitors, as the entrance is easily overlooked. This is the riverside cafe, where a cup of tea and a bun would set you back all of 6d.

BELPER, CRICH LANE 1955 B437031
In the 1850s Belper was selected as the headquarters for Derbyshire's first County Police Force under the provisions of the 1856 Police Act. Somewhat surprisingly, many millowners opposed its formation, preferring instead to keep their own private militias over which they exercised control. Or perhaps they were too tight fisted to contribute to the police rate to pay for 156 officers and men.

AMBERGATE, THE STATION C1955 A203017
The original North Midland Railway station at Amber Gate, as it was then called, was designed in the Jacobean style by NMR architect Francis Thompson and built in 1839. Renamed Ambergate in November 1846, it was replaced by a new station in 1863; this in turn was superseded by the famous triangular station in 1876.

AMBERGATE, THE STATION c1955 A203023A
A Manchester-bound train pulls out of Ambergate. The station survives as an unmanned halt, the connecting lines between the Sheffield and former Manchester routes having been removed. This view looks towards Matlock. The road on the right is the A610 to Ripley, and on the left is the Hurt Arms which was extensively rebuilt during 1998.

CROMFORD, THE BRIDGE 1886 18578

The 15th century bridge at Cromford is probably the oldest in the county, save for some of the sections of the causeway at Swarkestone. An unusual though not unique feature is that on one side there are round arches, and on the other they are pointed. This is due to one side of the bridge being rebuilt when the roadway was widened.

CROMFORD, THE BRIDGE 1892 31293

Partially hidden in the trees is an 18th century fishing temple almost identical to the one in Beresford Dale which was used by Isaac Walton and Charles Cotton. Cotton built his temple in 1674, and it was he who added chapters to the fifth edition of Walton's 'Compleat Angler'. Walton was also a biographer, whose subjects included John Donne (1640) and George Herbert (1670).

CROMFORD
The Greyhound Hotel 1892 31290A

Cromford was a secluded hamlet, home to a few lead miners and stockingers, until chosen by Richard Arkwright in 1772 as the site for his water-powered cotton mill. The Greyhound Hotel was built in 1778 for the benefit of visitors to Arkwright's mill. Though Arkwright also built cottages, a school and a church, he ruled the place like a feudal lord.

CROMFORD, WILLERSLEY CASTLE 1892 31292

CROMFORD
Willersley Castle 1892
Sir Richard Arkwright built Willersley Castle for his own use, but he died in 1792 before it was completed. The castle remained in the family for several generations and during the Great War was used as a convalescent home for troops. Later it was converted for use as a Methodist college and guest house.

◆

CROMFORD
Willersley Castle 1884
There is an inscription on the bridge that records the successful leaping of the parapet by a horse and rider in 1697. The bridge carried the principal road in the area, the Nottingham to Newhaven turnpike, over the river; then around 1818 a new valley road was completed along Matlock Dale.

CROMFORD, WILLERSLEY CASTLE 1884 16573

CROMFORD, WILLERSLEY CASTLE c1955 C193012

The creation of the parkland around Willersley Castle resulted in the old packhorse trail from Matlock Dale to Holloway and Cromford being closed. To provide an alternative route for packhorses into and out of Matlock Dale, Arkwright had the cliffs at Cromford Market Place blown up and a road, part of the present A6, cut through.

CROMFORD, LEA HURST 1892 31296
Lea Hurst was once the home of Florence Nightingale's family; it was they who opened the textile mill here that was eventually bought by John Smedley of Matlock. Nearby are Lea Gardens, which were established in the mid-20th century in a worked-out quarry. The gardens have over 500 species of rhododendrons growing there.

CROMFORD, THE BLACK ROCKS 1892 31294
The Black Rocks are a gritstone outcrop at Bolehill, near the summit of the steep hill out of Cromford on the road to Wirksworth, and have been a tourist attraction for decades. A bole hill was a method of smelting lead ore and is explained in a little more detail in the introduction.

ILKESTON, BATH STREET C1955 I37040
Ilkeston is said to derive its name from Elcha, a 7th century pirate; after sailing up the Humber on a raid he decided to settle in east Derbyshire. Elcha built a defensive earthwork called a tun, hence Elkeston. Ilkeston's population increased dramatically during the 1850s as new collieries were opened in the area; similar things were happening at Langley Mill and Eastwood.

ILKESTON, TOWN CENTRE c1955 I37059
The town's charter was granted by John of Gaunt in 1252, one of the privileges being a right to claim a 50% reduction on rents paid at any other market or fair. The right was to continue for as long as Ilkeston maintained a set of gallows.

ILKESTON, THE TENNIS COURTS c1955 I37024
In the 18th century a number of parishes got together and built a joint workhouse in an effort to cut expenditure on poor relief. However, such places were not always a success; some parishes simply welshed on their contributions. In 1779 the Ilkeston workhouse was demolished as it was empty and local authorities didn't like spending money on it.

ILKESTON, THE PARISH CHURCH c1955 137063
The tower of the old parish church of St Mary's was all but destroyed during a hurricane in 1714, but over twenty years went by before it was rebuilt. In 1855 the church suffered a restoration at the hands of the Victorians that amounted to a wholesale rebuild, though the tombs of Nicholas de Cantelupe, first lord of Ilkeston, and his son William were spared.

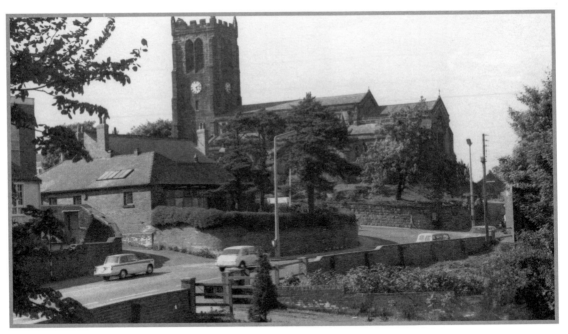

HEANOR, THE CHURCH c1955 H331014
In 1868 St Michael's Church was extensively rebuilt, with only the 15th century west tower surviving from the original structure. The tower itself appears to have been rebuilt around 1473-74 when the church was given to Dale Abbey who retained it until the Dissolution.

HEANOR, THE MEMORIAL AND THE CHURCH c1955 H331123
The church was once famed for its stained glass. In 1662 Sir William Dugdale of the College of Arms paid a visit and recorded that 'in the uppermost south window are two armed knights standing face to face and holding up these two Coates of Arms ...' By 1710 only six coats of arms survived: now there are none.

HEANOR, MARKET PLACE C1955 H331125
An old market town, Heanor was one of several north-east Derbyshire towns to be granted a market charter during the 13th century, which it gained nine years before either Alfreton or Ilkeston. With the advent of motor omnibuses, the Market Place also served as the local bus station; the town even used to have its own bus operator, Williamsons, but they were taken over in 1929 by Midland General.

HEANOR, THE MEMORIAL GARDENS c1955 H331007

HEANOR
The Memorial Gardens c1955

The war memorial gardens provided the inhabitants with an open space in the town centre. Heanor showed a little more thought in paying tribute to its war dead than most Derbyshire towns, where cenotaphs and memorials tend to stand cold and square in market places. It is said that at the end of the Great War there was a plan to give every war grave a marble headstone, but the project was abandoned because of the cost.

◆

HEANOR
The Memorial Gardens c1955

In the 1950s the memorial gardens appeared to be a favourite spot for mothers to get away from the housework for a while and give themselves and the kids a breath of fresh air.

HEANOR, THE MEMORIAL GARDENS c1955 H331127

HEANOR, THE PADDLING POOL c1955 H331004

In the 1950s most towns managed to provide a paddling pool for youngsters and Heanor was no different. Were the summers hotter then, or were children made of sterner stuff? Whatever the reason the place was certainly popular.

RIPLEY, MARKET PLACE c1955 R299042

As towns like Alfreton and Ripley increased their populations through immigrants seeking work in the mines, rural areas suffered falling population. In 1891 the villages of Breadsall, Elvaston and Kirk Langley had populations of 571, 519 and 613 respectively. By 1901 they had fallen to 515, 495 and 531.

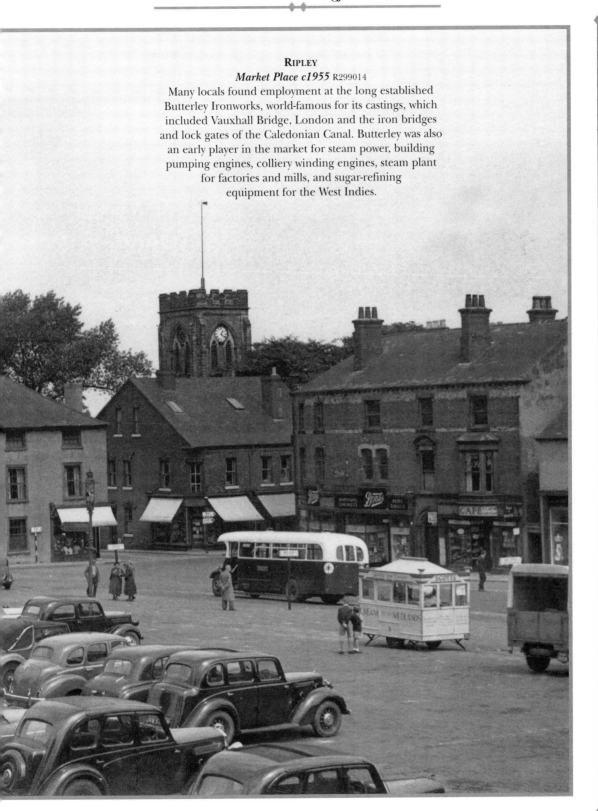

RIPLEY

Market Place c1955 R299014

Many locals found employment at the long established
Butterley Ironworks, world-famous for its castings, which
included Vauxhall Bridge, London and the iron bridges
and lock gates of the Caledonian Canal. Butterley was also
an early player in the market for steam power, building
pumping engines, colliery winding engines, steam plant
for factories and mills, and sugar-refining
equipment for the West Indies.

RIPLEY, CHURCH STREET c1955 R299018

The road to the left leads to Butterley, and to the right is the A610 to Nottingham. As with other towns of this size, the high street stores were present. On the left we have Woolworths and a small branch of Burtons.

RIPLEY, GROSVENOR ROAD c1955 R299020

This photograph was taken in the great pre-supermarket days when people had never heard of the catch phrase 'convenience shopping'.

Ripley, All Saints' Church c1955 R299039
Pentrich was once the mother church for the people of Ripley, who went to their devotions walking along a corpse-way, known locally as Dead Man's Lane. At the time of the Domesday survey, Ripley and Pentrich were assessed together; their combined value to the crown before 1066 was £4, and in 1085 it was down to 50s.

RIPLEY, NEW STREET c1965 R299045
Judging by the signs on Priestleys, the Japanese electronics industry still had to make its mark in the UK in the mid-sixties; in 1965 Daihatsu became the first-ever Japanese motor manufacturer to import cars, when their under-powered Compagno proved a disaster. Another sign of the times was the television aerials; you needed different ones for BBC and ITV.

RIPLEY, BUTTERLEY RESERVOIR c1955 R299009
Butterley Reservoir has been popular with anglers for many years. The tracks of the Midland Railway Project Centre now run alongside the reservoir, using part of the former Midland route between Ambergate and Codnor Park. The original Butterley station closed to passenger traffic in June 1947 and to goods in November 1964, though some private sidings remained in use.

RIPLEY, BUTTERLEY LIFT PARK c1965 R299062
This unique and strange-looking contraption stood near Butterley Ironworks and was an interesting attempt to find a way of parking a reasonable number of cars in a limited space. In 1811 Butterley became the first company in the East Midlands coalfield to build a new village for its workers. About 67 acres of meadowland were acquired in Alfreton parish, and Ironville was born.

ALFRETON
King Street c1955 A199015
By the beginning of the 11th century the town was known as
Aelfredington, becoming Alfreton by 1236. In 1801 the population
stood at 2000, and within sixty years had risen to around 26,000.
By 1921 Alfreton was the fifth largest town in the county.

ALFRETON, HIGH STREET c1955 A199016

On the left is the Odeon, built in the half-timbered style favoured by the company for many of its cinemas; the Odeon in Holywell Street, Chesterfield was another example. Across the road we have the usual high street chain stores of F W Woolworth and Burtons.

ALFRETON, HIGH STREET c1955 A199017

During the 17th century coal mining began to develop into an important industry in north-east Derbyshire, with pits around Smalley and Heanor. By the Napoleonic Wars local collieries were supplying Riddings ironworks. In those days skilled founders at Riddings earned from 3s to 5s a day, labourers between 1s 8d and 2s 4d a day and colliers from 2s 6d to 4s 6d a day.

ALFRETON, HIGH STREET c1960 A199023
Looking towards what has become a busy and often congested junction with the A61 Clay Cross to Swanwick road.

ALFRETON, WINGFIELD ROAD c1955 A199027
The opening of the Dukeries coalfield at the end of the Great War saw the development of the first generation of highly mechanised super pits. The populations of former rural villages such as Edwinstowe rocked with the influx of miners and their families. About 25 per cent of the immigrants to the coalfield came from Derbyshire, many from Alfreton, Ripley, Heanor and Codnor.

Index

Derby

Around Derby

Frith Book Co Titles

www.francisfrith.co.uk

The Frith Book Company publishes over 100 new titles each year. A selection of those currently available are listed below. For latest catalogue please contact Frith Book Co.

Town Books 96pages, approx 100 photos. County and Themed Books 128pages, approx 150 photos (unless specified). All titles hardback laminated case and jacket except those indicated pb (paperback)

Ancient Monuments & Stone Circles		
	1-85937-143-4	£17.99
Aylesbury (pb)	1-85937-227-9	£9.99
Bakewell	1-85937-113-2	£12.99
Barnstaple (pb)	1-85937-300-3	£9.99
Bath	1-85937-097-7	£12.99
Bedford (pb)	1-85937-205-8	£9.99
Berkshire (pb)	1-85937-191-4	£9.99
Berkshire Churches	1-85937-170-1	£17.99
Bognor Regis (pb)	1-85937-431-x	£9.99
Bournemouth	1-85937-067-5	£12.99
Bradford (pb)	1-85937-204-x	£9.99
Brighton & Hove(pb)	1-85937-192-2	£8.99
Bristol (pb)	1-85937-264-3	£9.99
British Life A Century Ago (pb)	1-85937-213-9	£9.99
Buckinghamshire (pb)	1-85937-200-7	£9.99
Camberley (pb)	1-85937-222-8	£9.99
Cambridge (pb)	1-85937-422-0	£9.99
Cambridgeshire (pb)	1-85937-420-4	£9.99
Canals & Waterways (pb)	1-85937-291-0	£9.99
Canterbury Cathedral (pb)	1-85937-179-5	£9.99
Cardiff (pb)	1-85937-093-4	£9.99
Carmarthenshire	1-85937-216-3	£14.99
Cheltenham (pb)	1-85937-095-0	£9.99
Cheshire (pb)	1-85937-271-6	£9.99
Chester	1-85937-090-x	£12.99
Chesterfield	1-85937-071-3	£9.99
Chichester (pb)	1-85937-228-7	£9.99
Colchester (pb)	1-85937-188-4	£8.99
Cornish Coast	1-85937-163-9	£14.99
Cornwall (pb)	1-85937-229-5	£9.99
Cornwall Living Memories	1-85937-248-1	£14.99
Cotswolds (pb)	1-85937-230-9	£9.99
Cotswolds Living Memories	1-85937-255-4	£14.99
County Durham	1-85937-123-x	£14.99
Cumbria	1-85937-101-9	£14.99
Dartmoor	1-85937-145-0	£14.99
Derbyshire (pb)	1-85937-196-5	£9.99
Devon (pb)	1-85937-297-x	£9.99
Dorset (pb)	1-85937-269-4	£9.99
Dorset Churches	1-85937-172-8	£17.99
Dorset Coast (pb)	1-85937-299-6	£9.99

Dorset Living Memories	1-85937-210-4	£14.99
Down the Severn	1-85937-118-3	£14.99
Down the Thames (pb)	1-85937-278-3	£9.99
Dublin (pb)	1-85937-231-7	£9.99
East Anglia (pb)	1-85937-265-1	£9.99
East London	1-85937-080-2	£14.99
East Sussex	1-85937-130-2	£14.99
Eastbourne	1-85937-061-6	£12.99
Edinburgh (pb)	1-85937-193-0	£8.99
English Castles (pb)	1-85937-434-4	£9.99
English Country Houses	1-85937-161-2	£17.99
Exeter	1-85937-126-4	£12.99
Exmoor	1-85937-132-9	£14.99
Falmouth	1-85937-066-7	£12.99
Folkestone (pb)	1-85937-124-8	£9.99
Glasgow (pb)	1-85937-190-6	£9.99
Gloucestershire	1-85937-102-7	£14.99
Greater Manchester (pb)	1-85937-266-x	£9.99
Hampshire Churches (pb)	1-85937-207-4	£9.99
Harrogate	1-85937-423-9	£9.99
Hastings & Bexhill (pb)	1-85937-131-0	£9.99
Heart of Lancashire (pb)	1-85937-197-3	£9.99
Helston (pb)	1-85937-214-7	£9.99
Hereford (pb)	1-85937-175-2	£9.99
Herefordshire	1-85937-174-4	£14.99
Humberside	1-85937-215-5	£14.99
Hythe, Romney Marsh & Ashford	1-85937-256-2	£9.99
Ipswich (pb)	1-85937-424-7	£9.99
Ireland (pb)	1-85937-181-7	£9.99
Isles of Scilly	1-85937-136-1	£14.99
Isle of Wight (pb)	1-85937-429-8	£9.99
Isle of Wight Living Memories	1-85937-304-6	£14.99
Kent (pb)	1-85937-189-2	£9.99
Kent Living Memories	1-85937-125-6	£14.99
Lake District (pb)	1-85937-275-9	£9.99
Lancaster, Morecambe & Heysham (pb)		
	1-85937-233-3	£9.99
Leeds (pb)	1-85937-202-3	£9.99
Leicester	1-85937-073-x	£12.99
Leicestershire (pb)	1-85937-185-x	£9.99
Lighthouses	1-85937-257-0	£17.99
Lincolnshire (pb)	1-85937-433-6	£9.99

Available from your local bookshop or from the publisher

Frith Book Co Titles (continued)

Liverpool & Merseyside (pb)	1-85937-234-1	£9.99	Southampton (pb)	1-85937-427-1	£9.99
London (pb)	1-85937-183-3	£9.99	Southport (pb)	1-85937-425-5	£9.99
Ludlow (pb)	1-85937-176-0	£9.99	Stratford upon Avon	1-85937-098-5	£12.99
Luton (pb)	1-85937-235-x	£9.99	Suffolk (pb)	1-85937-221-x	£9.99
Manchester (pb)	1-85937-198-1	£9.99	Suffolk Coast	1-85937-259-7	£14.99
New Forest	1-85937-128-0	£14.99	Surrey (pb)	1-85937-240-6	£9.99
Newport, Wales (pb)	1-85937-258-9	£9.99	Sussex (pb)	1-85937-184-1	£9.99
Newquay (pb)	1-85937-421-2	£9.99	Swansea (pb)	1-85937-167-1	£9.99
Norfolk (pb)	1-85937-195-7	£9.99	Tees Valley & Cleveland	1-85937-211-2	£14.99
Norfolk Living Memories	1-85937-217-1	£14.99	Thanet (pb)	1-85937-116-7	£9.99
Northamptonshire	1-85937-150-7	£14.99	Tiverton (pb)	1-85937-178-7	£9.99
Northumberland Tyne & Wear (pb)	1-85937-281-3	£9.99	Torbay	1-85937-063-2	£12.99
North Devon Coast	1-85937-146-9	£14.99	Truro	1-85937-147-7	£12.99
North Devon Living Memories	1-85937-261-9	£14.99	Victorian and Edwardian Cornwall	1-85937-252-x	£14.99
North Wales (pb)	1-85937-298-8	£9.99	Victorian & Edwardian Devon	1-85937-253-8	£14.99
North Yorkshire (pb)	1-85937-236-8	£9.99	Victorian & Edwardian Kent	1-85937-149-3	£14.99
Norwich (pb)	1-85937-194-9	£8.99	Vic & Ed Maritime Album	1-85937-144-2	£17.99
Nottingham (pb)	1-85937-324-0	£9.99	Victorian and Edwardian Sussex	1-85937-157-4	£14.99
Nottinghamshire (pb)	1-85937-187-6	£9.99	Victorian & Edwardian Yorkshire	1-85937-154-x	£14.99
Peak District (pb)	1-85937-280-5	£9.99	Victorian Seaside	1-85937-159-0	£17.99
Penzance	1-85937-069-1	£12.99	Villages of Devon (pb)	1-85937-293-7	£9.99
Peterborough (pb)	1-85937-219-8	£9.99	Villages of Kent (pb)	1-85937-294-5	£9.99
Piers	1-85937-237-6	£17.99	Warwickshire (pb)	1-85937-203-1	£9.99
Plymouth	1-85937-119-1	£12.99	Welsh Castles (pb)	1-85937-322-4	£9.99
Poole & Sandbanks (pb)	1-85937-251-1	£9.99	West Midlands (pb)	1-85937-289-9	£9.99
Preston (pb)	1-85937-212-0	£9.99	West Sussex	1-85937-148-5	£14.99
Reading (pb)	1-85937-238-4	£9.99	West Yorkshire (pb)	1-85937-201-5	£9.99
Salisbury (pb)	1-85937-239-2	£9.99	Weymouth (pb)	1-85937-209-0	£9.99
St Ives	1-85937-068-3	£12.99	Wiltshire (pb)	1-85937-277-5	£9.99
Scotland (pb)	1-85937-182-5	£9.99	Wiltshire Churches (pb)	1-85937-171-x	£9.99
Scottish Castles (pb)	1-85937-323-2	£9.99	Wiltshire Living Memories	1-85937-245-7	£14.99
Sheffield, South Yorks (pb)	1-85937-267-8	£9.99	Winchester (pb)	1-85937-428-x	£9.99
Shrewsbury (pb)	1-85937-325-9	£9.99	Windmills & Watermills	1-85937-242-2	£17.99
Shropshire (pb)	1-85937-326-7	£9.99	Worcestershire	1-85937-152-3	£14.99
Somerset	1-85937-153-1	£14.99	York (pb)	1-85937-199-x	£9.99
South Devon Coast	1-85937-107-8	£14.99	Yorkshire (pb)	1-85937-186-8	£9.99
South Devon Living Memories	1-85937-168-x	£14.99	Yorkshire Living Memories	1-85937-166-3	£14.99
South Hams	1-85937-220-1	£14.99			

Frith Book Co titles available soon

1880's England	Oct 01	1-85937-331-3	£17.99	Gloucester (pb)	Oct 01	1-85937-417-4	£9.99
Amersham & Chesham (pb)	Oct 01	1-85937-340-2	£9.99	Oxfordshire (pb)	Oct 01	1-85937-430-1	£9.99
Bedfordshire	Oct 01	1-85937-320-8	£14.99	Picturesque Harbours	Oct 01	1-85937-208-2	£17.99
Belfast (pb)	Oct 01	1-85937-303-8	£9.99	Romford (pb)	Oct 01	1-85937-319-4	£9.99
Britain Living Memories	Oct 01	1-85937-343-7	£17.99	Worcester (pb)	Oct 01	1-85937-165-5	£9.99
Chelmsford (pb)	Oct 01	1-85937-310-0	£9.99	Villages of Sussex (pb)	Oct 01	1-85937-295-3	£9.99

See Frith books on the internet www.francisfrith.co.uk

FRITH PRODUCTS & SERVICES

Francis Frith would doubtless be pleased to know that the pioneering publishing venture he started in 1860 still continues today. A hundred and forty years later, The Francis Frith Collection continues in the same innovative tradition and is now one of the foremost publishers of vintage photographs in the world. Some of the current activities include:

Interior Decoration

Today Frith's photographs can be seen framed and as giant wall murals in thousands of pubs, restaurants, hotels, banks, retail stores and other public buildings throughout the country. In every case they enhance the unique local atmosphere of the places they depict and provide reminders of gentler days in an increasingly busy and frenetic world.

Product Promotions

Frith products are used by many major companies to promote the sales of their own products or to reinforce their own history and heritage. Frith promotions have been used by Hovis bread, Courage beers, Scots Porage Oats, Colman's mustard, Cadbury's foods, Mellow Birds coffee, Dunhill pipe tobacco, Guinness, and Bulmer's Cider.

Genealogy and Family History

As the interest in family history and roots grows world-wide, more and more people are turning to Frith's photographs of Great Britain for images of the towns, villages and streets where their ancestors lived; and, of course, photographs of the churches and chapels where their ancestors were christened, married and buried are an essential part of every genealogy tree and family album.

Frith Products

All Frith photographs are available Framed or just as Mounted Prints and Posters (size 23 x 16 inches). These may be ordered from the address below. From time to time other products - Address Books, Calendars, Table Mats, etc - are available.

The Internet

Already twenty thousand Frith photographs can be viewed and purchased on the internet through the Frith websites and a myriad of partner sites.

For more detailed information on Frith companies and products, look at these sites:

www.francisfrith.co.uk
www.francisfrith.com
(for North American visitors)

See the complete list of Frith Books at:

www.francisfrith.co.uk

This web site is regularly updated with the latest list of publications from the Frith Book Company. If you wish to buy books relating to another part of the country that your local bookshop does not stock, you may purchase on-line.

For further information, trade, or author enquiries please contact us at the address below:
The Francis Frith Collection, Frith's Barn, Teffont, Salisbury, Wiltshire, England SP3 5QP.
Tel: +44 (0)1722 716 376 Fax: +44 (0)1722 716 881 Email: sales@francisfrith.co.uk

See Frith books on the internet www.francisfrith.co.uk

TO RECEIVE YOUR **FREE** MOUNTED PRINT

Mounted Print
Overall size 14 x 11 inches

Cut out this Voucher and return it with your remittance for £1.95 to cover postage and handling, to UK addresses. For overseas addresses please include £4.00 post and handling. Choose any photograph included in this book. Your SEPIA print will be A4 in size, and mounted in a cream mount with burgundy rule line, overall size 14 x 11 inches.

Order additional Mounted Prints at HALF PRICE (only £7.49 each*)

If there are further pictures you would like to order, possibly as gifts for friends and family, purchase them at half price (no additional postage and handling required).

Have your Mounted Prints framed*

For an additional £14.95 per print you can have your chosen Mounted Print framed in an elegant polished wood and gilt moulding, overall size 16 x 13 inches (no additional postage and handling required).

---

* IMPORTANT!
These special prices are only available if ordered using the original voucher on this page (no copies permitted) and at the same time as your free Mounted Print, for delivery to the same address

---

Frith Collectors' Guild

From time to time we publish a magazine of news and stories about Frith photographs and further special offers of Frith products. If you would like 12 months FREE membership, please return this form.

Send completed forms to:
The Francis Frith Collection, Frith's Barn, Teffont, Salisbury, Wiltshire SP3 5QP

Voucher for **FREE** and Reduced Price Frith Prints

Picture no.	Page number	Qty	Mounted @ £7.49	Framed + £14.95	Total Cost
		1	Free of charge*	£	£
			£7.49	£	£
			£7.49	£	£
			£7.49	£	£
			£7.49	£	£
			£7.49	£	£

Please allow 28 days for delivery	*** Post & handling**	**£1.95**
Book Title	**Total Order Cost**	**£**

Please do not photocopy this voucher. Only the original is valid, so please cut it out and return it to us.

I enclose a cheque / postal order for £ . . . . made payable to 'The Francis Frith Collection' OR please debit my Mastercard / Visa / Switch / Amex card *(credit cards please on all overseas orders)*

Number . . . .

Issue No(Switch only) . . . . .Valid from (Amex/Switch) . . . .

Expires . . . . Signature . . . .

Name Mr/Mrs/Ms . . . .

Address . . . .

. . . .

. . . . Postcode . . . .

Daytime Tel No . . . .   Valid to 31/12/02

The Francis Frith Collectors' Guild

Please enrol me as a member for 12 months free of charge.

Name Mr/Mrs/Ms . . . .

Address . . . .

. . . .

. . . . Postcode . . . .

Would you like to find out more about Francis Frith?

We have recently recruited some entertaining speakers who are happy to visit local groups, clubs and societies to give an illustrated talk documenting Frith's travels and photographs. If you are a member of such a group and are interested in hosting a presentation, we would love to hear from you.

Our speakers bring with them a small selection of our local town and county books, together with sample prints. They are happy to take orders. A small proportion of the order value is donated to the group who have hosted the presentation. The talks are therefore an excellent way of fundraising for small groups and societies.

Can you help us with information about any of the Frith photographs in this book?

We are gradually compiling an historical record for each of the photographs in the Frith archive. It is always fascinating to find out the names of the people shown in the pictures, as well as insights into the shops, buildings and other features depicted.

If you recognize anyone in the photographs in this book, or if you have information not already included in the author's caption, do let us know. We would love to hear from you, and will try to publish it in future books or articles.

Our production team

Frith books are produced by a small dedicated team at offices in the converted Grade II listed 18th-century barn at Teffont near Salisbury, illustrated above. Most have worked with the Frith Collection for many years. All have in common one quality: they have a passion for the Frith Collection. The team is constantly expanding, but currently includes:

Jason Buck, John Buck, Heather Crisp, Isobel Hall, Rob Hames, Hazel Heaton, Peter Horne, James Kinnear, Tina Leary, Eliza Sackett, Terence Sackett, Sandra Sanger, Shelley Tolcher, Susanna Walker, Clive Wathen, Jenny Wathen and Douglas Burns.